MY SEABORGIUM

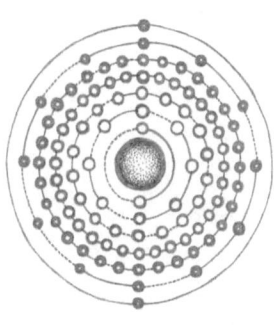

Other titles by Alicia Rebecca Myers

Greener

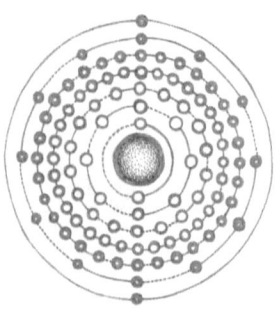

The Mineral Point Poetry Series

Tanka & Me   Kaethe Schwehn
My Seaborgium   Alicia Rebecca Myers
Fair Day in an Ancient Town   Greg Allendorf
My Tall Handsome   Emily Corwin

MINERAL POINT POETRY SERIES NO. 2
Kiki Petrosino, Editor

MY SEABORGIUM

Alicia Rebecca Myers

poems

Brain Mill Press · Green Bay, Wisconsin

Some of these poems have appeared previously in the following publications:

Gulf Coast: "Addling"

jubilat: "The Untelling"

The Fairy Tale Review: "Legs"

jdbrecords: "Inside the Grotesquery"

Best New Poets 2015: "The Last Travel Agent"

The Carolina Quarterly: "Canary Be Attendant" and "15 Weeks"

The American Literary Review: "24 Weeks," "33/34 Weeks," "39 Weeks"

Emotive Fruition and Radiolab: Elemental Poetry for the Masses: "Lullaby"

Stone Canoe: "Song for Distance"

The author would like to thank the Kimmel Harding Nelson Center for the Arts. Several of the poems in this book were completed while in residency.

Copyright © 2016 by Alicia Rebecca Myers. All rights reserved.
ISBN 978-1-942083-14-6

Cover photograph © Lacey Jones.
Cover design by Stray King Design.
Interior illustration by Ann O'Connell.
Interior design by Williams Writing, Editing & Design.

www.brainmillpress.com

The Mineral Point Poetry Series, number 2.

Published by Brain Mill Press, the Mineral Point Series is edited by Kiki Petrosino. In odd years, the series invites submissions of poetry chapbooks around a theme. In even years, the editor chooses a full collection.

for Miles

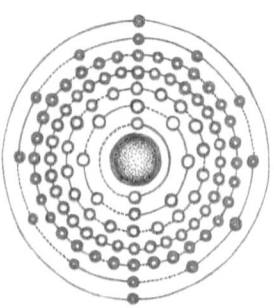

Contents

Foreword   *ix*

Hostess   *1*

I   LAND/LOSS
Addling   *5*
The Untelling   *6*
Legs   *7*
Inside the Grotesquery   *9*
The Last Travel Agent   *11*
Canary Be Attendant   *12*

II   WATER/WAIT
15 Weeks   *15*
24 Weeks   *16*
Chorus   *17*
33/34 Weeks   *18*
39 Weeks   *19*
Linnet   *20*

III   AIR/HERE
Cedar Waxwing   *23*
Harmers' Market   *24*
In the Hall of Mammals,
Your Young Fur Thickens   *25*

Duet, 2035 *26*
Lullaby *27*
Song for Distance *28*

About the Author *29*
Credits *31*

Foreword

Seaborgium is a synthetic element. It didn't even exist until 1974, when scientists invented a machine that could bombard atoms of one element with atoms of another. The most stable isotope of Seaborgium has a half-life of just two minutes. So far, there are no practical uses for this substance, except perhaps to mark for us a "before" and an "after." Once upon a time, there was no such thing as Seaborgium. Now, there is.

"If what happens after we die is the same as / what happened before then what / must count is the middle," Alicia Rebecca Myers claims in her prefatory poem. In this series of remarkable meditations, time collapses. Personal histories and fairytales become endlessly permeable, bombarding one another like the atoms that comprise Seaborgium. "Like the cream filling / in a Twinkie how did I get here?" Myers's speaker asks, and in this chapbook, "here" unfolds as a collage of love's mysterious "middles": a quotidian moment of observing one's child at play ("Hostess"); a memory of the speaker as a child, observing her father destroy a nest of goose eggs ("Addling"); that same speaker grieving a lost pregnancy ("The Untelling") and exulting in childbirth ("Linnet"). These poems remind us that every moment resonates multidirectionally in the long process of becoming.

In an interview, the poet Sharon Olds describes her relationship to metaphor this way:

> I don't know that metaphor helps understanding as much as it is a release into a different realm of one's understanding.

For Olds, metaphors emerge as artifacts of attentive play:

> I think there's a way that my brain wants to play while it's working and wants to escape the present but then it escapes by running off and playing. And then it brings back what it has found in play, which has some kind of beauty to it. . . .

As with Olds's work, the poems of *My Seaborgium* utilize metaphor in an attempt to account for the beauty that emerges from our moments of greatest grief. This work focuses on the (often unspoken) hardships of womanhood: miscarriage and infertility; the dangers of childbirth; the yearning to surpass society's narrow expectations of a woman's path to fulfillment in life. But despite (even: *because of*) the seriousness of the subject matter, this is a project that requires linguistic playfulness, keen observation, and musical acuity. Even through the pain, Myers's speaker struggles to pay attention, to unfold that pain in ways that feel particular and personal.

A poem like "Harmers' Market," for example, draws us in with its wry pun of a title, making us question, along with the speaker, the commercial-minded "biddies of disease" who sell memorial trinkets instead of cures and "kale." The market becomes a metaphor for our contemporary moment, revealing that despite the wisdom supposedly available through technology and our capitalistic purchasing power, we're still individually helpless before the larger mysteries of life and death.

With this in mind, the poems' occasional allusions to fairytales—linguistic repositories of collective wisdom—make sense. Myers addresses *faerie* as a chance to interrogate how women's desire is problematized, dismissed, and even forgotten in traditional tales. In "Legs," we meet Hans Christian Andersen's mermaid just after she trades her beautiful voice for a pair of legs she doesn't yet know how to use. "What was it about / legs that she'd wanted so badly [. . .] something to do with the soul," Myers's mermaid wonders. Her moment of amnesia is profound but not complete; language is still there, the lifeline she uses to lead herself out of despair.

In concluding the poem with her mermaid's silent prayer, Myers suggests that women's voices must never disappear, even if society does not always want to hear from them. The crucial, interior work continues in luminous language. "Dear Lord   Dear Liege   Dear Legs," the mermaid prays, and her wordplay brings our focus back to the female body, back to the mysterious wellspring of "after" and "before."

                      Kiki Petrosino
                      Editor, Mineral Point Poetry Series

MY SEABORGIUM

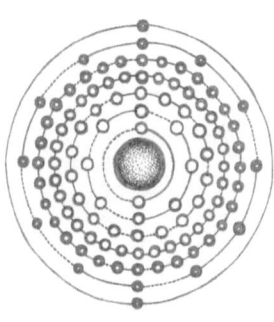

Hostess

If what happens after we die is the same as
what happened before then what
must count is the middle. Like the cream filling
in a Twinkie how did I get here?
I watch you practicing skills.
I could swoop and holler
till the cows sidle up
to your chub. Here is the church, here is
the crutch of my body keeping
you horizontal only
so long. Hello, how many
in your party? Once in your high chair
it's drop giraffe get giraffe ad
nauseam. Draw me a bath
of dissolvable packing peanuts
and later, I'll tell you the story of how
I rolled around in a mail truck full of other
people's letters, I was that happy
to be your mother.

I
LAND / LOSS

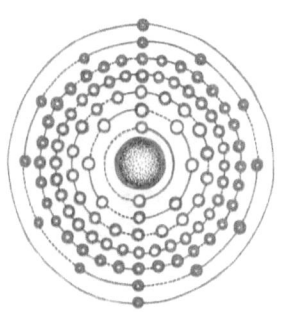

Addling

My father carried corn oil into dusk:
the translucent plastic like a lantern
held aloft, the yard pared down
immaculate—and overrun somehow
with a wild stamina. The light
was just ending. The geese were out,
feeding on the seeded grass. They lunged
the narrow slick of their bills
into the loam, weeded stalks
unmindful of the space between them,
the whites of their chinstraps
impellent, unrehearsed, in rhythm to collective
hunger and inner-directed. Larger
than each bird alone I watched my father:
his stooped shadow, his flannel untucked
like a lake spilling over its banks. He moved
outside their periphery until he was nothing more
than pine, a mere familiar. Then I watched him
unscrew the cap and pour oil onto cloth,
lower into a nest of moss and feathers,
into a clutch of eggs I couldn't see
but knew was there.
The geese continued to eat.
The eggs absorbed the oil.
I tried to pick out the mother
while my father asphyxiated embryos,
his head turned towards the gaggle in humane
say-so. I wanted to feel her bristle.
He said she'd be misled into believing
the eggs would develop. That not knowing,
she would tend to them the same.

The Untelling

I was a well and then I wasn't.
I shook a rainstick. It turned out to be a telescope.
I put it to my eye anyway, grew accustomed to distance.
A client writes to say he needs to go to Gnats, France.
You mean Nantes? I reply.
This uptick in luck was really just a fluke.
We're looking at what once was and where it once was.
That blithe star, whose light of death has reached us.
I must have said *this time* a dozen different times, just to
    take it back.
My barista asked why the sudden switch to decaf.
You ask if blue can be a naturally occurring color.
Maybe in stones, I say.
I lied when I told you that I didn't hide the egg timer.
The recipe called for jujube, not plum.
Summarily, my belly knew.

Legs

The ocean was popular and nearby removed
       from her like an ablation her grandmother
warned that she would be removed from *it* her body
                          excised from water
what happened was different

an emptying out   as if she'd contained all
along that which she'd lived in like a rainbow
in a portrait of a saint
      whose heart has been rent and   lifted

the patina of silent repetition
  deafening   first she touched toes to lips
an algae bloom of blood what was it about
legs that she'd wanted so badly   something to do
   with the soul   she could feel his soul against her chest
                   as he almost drowned
the thin cloud of it her almost soul on the temple floor
   straightening his legs like oars to scull her into eternity
                              genitalia
were nothing new tender pressure-center
in her tail   spot that shimmered in the phosphorescence
                              of yellow fin
        fusiliers   a school of them   darting
      in and out of hushed coral
                that only revealed its color
                      when in proximity

                to light she was light
with legs   what did it mean to live
            forever legs legs legs her knees were a rosary
she kissed morning noon and night but especially night
when God appeared a gelatinous eye
blinking a metronome demanding that she dance

  awake she felt the water pouring out
                    asleep the same
between her legs the memory of basin   nautilus
                            sharks as mammoth as sunken
                vessels   hydrothermal vents like chimneys
   migration sounds

once the surface of the ocean turned
        milky miles and miles of pale tundra she'd wished
                                that she could walk on
      more than walk   kneel
                        she'd wished that she could
                                        kneel before

such pure absolution examining the hole between her
   legs she wondered if this is where
the soul will enter
        when it does she wound
her braid she thought a prayer
                Dear Lord   Dear Liege   Dear Legs

Inside the Grotesquery

A little girl screams behind the castle.
Shhh a cricket hears
with its front legs. Once upon a time
everything above the sky
was water. Maybe in the bibbidi
kind was kinder. I'm storybooking
in threes, aren't you? I sell this
for a living. I called the preferred agent line
and got Perdita. No cigarette butts
in the parks like a million dead
stellar cores. I weld this
for the giving. The smell of citrus
wafts like noblesse oblige back to a simpler,
rounder time. Do not resuscitate.
Either Eeyore, or the illusion.
Sorcerer Mickey can control the stars and comets.
Mickey can't.
We have this grief in common.
A grandma shouldn't squeeze
into a trundle but
she'll try, she'll try.
People are cheap
and terrible. I've been known to exclaim
"Royal Table is the most important meal of all!"
If you wear your own costume please refrain
from signing autographs. Leave that to the real.
The summer I turned 19 I pulled order
tickets from a printer, served mouse-shaped
pizzas, wore purple polyester. Mark
in Maintenance asked to meet me
at the Polynesian. I'd only ever kissed.

I waited in a hammock.
The stars unlatched,
one by one. I've been offered
the survey hundreds of times. I'm afraid
I'm still on hold. Take back
this tiara. I want to be
Pizarro, dreaming
of Peru before he found it.

The Last Travel Agent

She hides honey in a globe.
Her hair smells of camphor.
Mornings, children scatter
heirlooms. Their fingers work the ash.
Here is a mesh of lace. Here is a rope
of felt. Sometimes the stones become the fragile
cups and saucers she once laid out for friends.
Remember the sky
strewn with paper lanterns?
The moon as anything other
than dread? O bird with one wing
heavier than the other.
Air splinters. Like a Medusa head
the capstan glowers.
Geography is spent.
Line them up, line them up.
How does the fable go again? Enough stones
in the pitcher and the crow can drink.

Canary Be Attendant

canary be attendant
through atrium   philter   glint
through wand and waves   boundary
be albedo   yellow lattice winged

cultivar I sat under
when child was just a thought
I heard the song   I taught it to him
spindle   iris   cord
invocation sung
together   canary sing in hollow

of my collarbone come perch   this plastic
    saint
tucked in my bra   this threaded
needle swinging   count
yourself among the couriers   carried
in the creel these charms
these charms
fall short

roll your watchful water sound   lullaby
stay what is wanted
stirrup   atlas   crown
trill us through
I've had enough of lilac   blood variations
day has formed   the sun
is composite
canary canary the heart's begun

II
WATER / WAIT

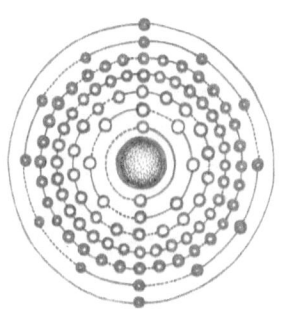

15 Weeks

Winter in Nebraska. Tiny floes skirr the river like translucent trash. Dark-eyed juncos peck the ground. *An eagle* Andrew says, and I wonder if she's ever swooped close enough to see a brass finial fashioned after her own likeness. Inside, the pressure of fructifying. I repeatedly wake at 3 AM, what Grandma Walker called the convict hour, when escaped men would break into your shotgun house to kill you. Hands noiseless as beargrass. I listen for the pitch of snow on windows. I haven't gotten past the fear that you're not alive. That the town will dredge you from my muddy body. Catfish barbels for hair. Slugs for ears. Last night I stumbled in the dim, ate toast by glow of the humidifier. The birders share their binoculars. Geoff tells us after years of marriage he's come to recognize his wife by sound alone: the rhythm of their broom on linoleum or her breath, seconds before a pit hits the sink. A mute woodpecker rams his head, a moshing rocker with red plumage. His retina protected by a second eyelid. I'm carrying spares, like Cami who buys two of everything she loves. Once at a party she wore the same watch on separate wrists. They told discrepant times. I want you to know the difference in music made by my walking with my head up and my head down. I click my tongue to transmit something vatic. I speak your name over and over directly to the center, your hollowest bone.

24 Weeks

Calving: to detach or give birth.
So as to be both drift and manifold.
The splinter inside the whorl.
I pinch-test my nipples to see if they lift
away from the breast. Success! I do this
while breaking coverage of the missing plane insists
no wreckage. Imagine standing on a mountain
and trying to spot a suitcase on the ground below.
Then imagine doing it in complete darkness.
Then imagine doing it with another's eyes
fused inside you. Not even recognizing
your own body. I open my mouth to the fluted stem
of a crape myrtle. More in bloom because
it was cut back. Because it was cut. My friend
is likewise hopeful in the pare of divorce.
We're told to detach makes birth manageable.

Chorus

The Argos cement truck
circles back a third time.
I've forgotten if the hundred eyes
were housed in one head
or many. These days I care so little
for myth, how witness works.
Now when I catch sight
of myself in windows of Last Resort
I deliberately extend my abdomen,
shine like a buffet
Buddha begging touch. I round out
like a hassock. I believe in God just so
I can revise:
hello Spry Fundus, hello
Winged Stria.
My memory of pain no more
than the memory of having once compared
a good apple to a good orange.
My own eyes, dazzling and compound.
Mornings, I outswim
women half my age. With a featherweight
heart I fold and refold
the layette, dream of kicks
from a fruitless chorus. I need them
behind me. To them I've upturned
my alms bowl. Hello Golden Reticulate,
hello Show. I've renamed
every leaf, every bereavement.

33/34 Weeks

I learn light behaves dually as wave and particle.
This *two-in-one* shampoo is *two-for-one*.
For your best interest.
In your best fortress.
At Folly Beach, my shadow shows in every frame.
Wasps bump dumbly between haint blue ceiling and sky.
Weight gain makes me question aviation.
I'm unsure of what's to come.
I bury my fingers in the hotel's ice bin, count backwards.
Pain tolerance isn't the same as pain threshold.
The Gullah women bundle their sweet grass.
Coiling their spoons in intricate circles.
I could both find and abandon you in a basket.
One foot in, one foot out.

39 Weeks

A comedian commits suicide.
An unarmed black teenager is gunned down.
I ready for the bloody show. Inside
our new house the cats sniff corners, ghost town
remnants of others. There's only before
and after. I uncover Queen Anne's lace
in the back of a Cheveret drawer,
bunched and curled, each dried floret like a face
repeating gestures, or a wicket door.
In a few days the delivery gown
I ordered from Pretty Pushers will grace
my body. Your misshapen head will crown
from the hidden world to the world laid bare,
hands splayed in surrender, saying: *I'm here.*

Linnet

Birth: radial. Becoming a starfish
growing a spine. Center of a mirror,
tarantella, this line of fire, this
tambourine tearing through. My insides: pain
like a double-handled saw bisecting
my lower back, bringing me back into
rocking. Then rhombic crystallization
of garnet. Gravity. Pressure, torch, or
arroyo (rain-filled promise). Whirligig.
Yaw. Ship carrying pearl ash purified
by kiln, this sea change, this delighting in
red skies, in freight. Glacial channel. Maw of
sliced open nacelle, loved layabout. This
calm, this room, this ohm, this not like being
held together by anything other
than gravity: fatigue song. Percussive.
Train headed into watercourse. Double-
sided psalm. Familiar mastery. Sway.
Turn. My breath fogging the glass
as a distant linnet gathers knotgrass
by the sea, to weave, to build a nest of
salt, of thistledown, to house the hunger
that will feed on flax, tiny seed from which
linen is made, starred cloth we wrap you in.

III
AIR/HERE

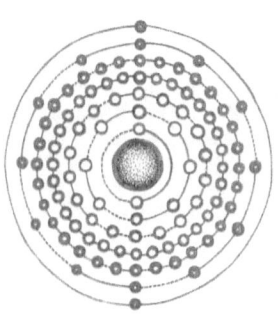

Cedar Waxwing

Caroline found a dead bird
on the shoulder of the road
and took it home to
paint from. No book comes close
to approximating the colors of a fresh
kill. The red-dipped wings,
the yellow-capped tail,
all seem juiced with
brush fire. I lift you up
in different lights to see
your skin diffuse. The days
repeat like tract houses
I want to live in. Those babies
in the magazines all have subfusc
cheeks. Better copy
of me, I do my best to illuminate
you, showcased by windows,
whisper *my model, my model.*

Harmers' Market

I seek out covert like a rare coin
collector. The biddies of disease,
wringing their hands behind
the kale. Tinderbox: they want
to twirl your locks into cylindrical
candies! I vow never to knot
you as a means to keep you. Love as
offensive, love as war paint
of dove's blood. Around every corner
the potential for a loose
scoreboard. I'm the lookout for
crooked carrot, iron owl. I rock you
in an Adirondack chair, far
from the cone snail.

In the Hall of Mammals, Your Young Fur Thickens

Extending westward with large eyes no nest-
site fidelity you
scrabble powder-downed
parts alert to the gouge, articulated:
crown to nerve to bone, split peg
and sinew, to flag, to hinge,
to hammer. Noisy climber,
strangely aerial, with claws
spread out against the skin against
the lungs. Chest vortices white
hot. Haunches primed in musk.
After you were born tree
meant more, root meant more, rocky-
footed ox you would destroy
even the most rare
Eskimo-carved ivory.

Duet, 2035

Not until retro karaoke hour
can I admit it. In profile, by drone,
we order beers. Peruse the beam. Power
ballads were my go-to then, Heart's "Alone,"
maybe a Pat Benatar hit. One drink
in and I slip. Spew about the first time
you flew, my infant in arms. We lip synch
to popular Alt Surveillance Rock. *Mom,*
you say. And just like that: the summery
haul of the nape of your neck. How long
since I held you? "Angel From Montgomery"
fills the sphere. *Mom, come on, just pick a song.*
You're all grown. "Dock of the Bay (Sittin' On)."
You offer to whistle a verse. My son.

Lullaby

Now I want joy to arrange you.
Forget the spool, the queue.
May you crow from the prow.
Be your element's namesake
and alive, know it. My Seaborgium.
My little radish bugaboo, my
pillowfoot jeweler. Sweetgum,
sing, sing to wake the water.

Song for Distance

I push the stroller up the hill
and each square of sidewalk marks a year
into your future, the good
exertion of it. Miles above sea level
a medium dangles her arm
out a car window. The wind takes her
bracelet. On the ride back she'll ask the dead
to tell her the exact ditch into which it
fell. She'll yell, *Pull over,* point.
I also beg direction of what's behind me.
How much do I love you?
This much, I say, arms outstretched in a yoga
    pose I named
Sleep Deprived Air Traffic Controller.
I'll never get the map
refolded right. Ditto for assembling
your furniture. For now, I set you
in a pen but Muffin, I'm shucking the oyster
as best I know how. You rouse
all hours. Rocket like the possessed,
clap hands or collapse into Tabletop
on autopilot. I look both ways before I cross.
I'm just now noticing the tops of things.
Every day is a day I can return to.

About the Author

Alicia Rebecca Myers is a poet and essayist whose work has appeared recently or is forthcoming in *The Rumpus, Brain Child Magazine, The American Literary Review, Best New Poets 2015, Gulf Coast, jubilat, The Carolina Quarterly,* and *The Fairy Tale Review.* In February 2014, she was awarded a residency at the Kimmel Harding Nelson Center in Nebraska City. A graduate of NYU's MFA Program, she currently teaches at Wells College. You can find her online at aliciarebeccamyers.com.

Credits

Author	Alicia Rebecca Myers
First Reader	My Dan Rosenberg
Editors	Kiki Petrosino, Ruthie Knox, and Mary Ann Rivers
Cover Photography	Lacey Jones
Cover Design	Stray King Design
Proofreader	Beaumont Hardy Editing
Interior Art	Ann O'Connell
Interior Design	Williams Writing, Editing & Design

Brain Mill Press would like to acknowledge the support of the following patrons:

Noelle Adams

Rhyll Biest

Katherine Bodsworth

Lea Franczak

Barry and Barbara Homrighaus

Kelly Lauer

Susan Lee

Sherri Marx

Aisling Murphy

Audra North

Molly O'Keefe

Virginia Parker

Cherri Porter

Erin Rathjen

Robin Drouin Tuch

www.ingramcontent.com/pod-product-compliance
Lightning Source LLC
Chambersburg PA
CBHW021453080526
44588CB00009B/831